THE *Girls' Guide* TO
GROWTH MINDSET

THE *Girls' Guide* TO GROWTH MINDSET

A Can-Do Approach to Building Confidence, Courage, and Grit

KENDRA COATES, D.ED.

ROCKRIDGE
PRESS

Interior and Cover Designer: Jennifer Hsu

Art Producer: Tom Hood

Editor: Erin Nelson

Production Editor: Nora Milman

Illustrations @ iStock/Nadezda_Grapes, cover and pp. xii, 9, 27, 35, 62, 74, 84, 95, 106, 109, 115, 118, 133 & 140; Creative Market/softulka pp. ii, iv, xiii, 15, 21, 37, 57, 78, 85, 90, 99, 116, 119, 123, 125, 129, 131, 143, 144, 146, 149 & 150; iStock/Ma_rish p. 4; iStock/Lesla_G p. 121

ISBN: Print 978-1-64611-056-8

R0

FOR ROUENE AND RIEDER,
WHO TEACH AND INSPIRE ME EVERY DAY
TO LIVE MY GROWTH MINDSET
AND SUPPORT THEM AS THEY LIVE THEIRS.

CONTENTS

WE DO NOT NEED

MAGIC

TO TRANSFORM OUR WORLD.

WE CARRY

ALL THE POWER WE NEED

INSIDE

OURSELVES ALREADY.

—J. K. ROWLING

INTRODUCTION

Did you know that you are full of power, right in this very moment? With your power, you learn, change, design, create, help, inspire, teach, and grow. You set and reach your goals and make your dreams come true. You change the world. You are today's and tomorrow's thinkers, learners, inventors, designers, changemakers, dream builders, and leaders.

So, where does this power come from? You are **malleable**, which means that you can change—you can learn anything you want. This power is always inside of you. You *are* power. So how are you going to use it?

This guide is a good place to start! You can think of these pages as a journey you're embarking on—a way to get to know yourself better. How you decide to put these words into action is up to you. You may decide to volunteer in your community, introduce yourself to someone new, join a sports team, audition for a role in a musical or play, join a science, technology, engineering, art, or mathematics (STEAM) club, design and organize a project, take on a leadership role at your school, march in the streets, learn a new instrument or language, or write a short story or book!

In this book, you will learn more about the power inside you and how to unlock it. Specifically, you'll:

* Practice curiosity and courage

* Increase your confidence

* Set goals and reach them

* Ask questions that inspire a new way of understanding

* Confidently share your ideas and opinions

* Better understand your thoughts and emotions

* Activate your creativity

* Take on safe and fun learning risks and challenges!

* Learn from your mistakes

* Have fun failing!

* Practice empathy

* Cultivate relationships with friends, family, and teachers

* Break old rules—and design new ones

* Reject outdated thinking

* Design and create your own path

Your possibilities are limitless. The vision you create along the way has no boundaries. Your adventure awaits!

What You'll Need

Are you ready? The most important thing you'll need—I bet you can guess—is YOU! To unlock your power, you'll need permission from yourself to go for it, to show up however you are in the moment. You'll need to practice kindness and patience toward yourself. You'll need a big supply of curiosity to ask questions. You'll need confidence and courage to be yourself. You'll need the bravery to explore new ways of thinking. And you'll need to get comfortable making mistakes. (Trust me, they're fun!)

One last thing you need to know is that this is a safe learning zone. It is judgment-free, and there are no evaluations. There is no wrong or right, and you don't need to prove anything to anyone. All are welcome!

If you want, grab a piece of paper and a pen, get your journal, or just write in your head. There are even some spaces for you to write in this book if inspiration strikes. Those who love and care about you want to learn with you, so when you're ready, think about sharing your journey with them. Ask them questions and share your thoughts and emotions as best you can.

A Note on Gender

This book is intended for anyone who identifies as a girl or young woman. Here you'll find support for all forms of girlhood and young womanhood. While I use the pronouns "she," "her," and "hers," the lessons here also apply to anyone whose pronouns are "they," "their," "he," "him," or any others. If you are a boy reading this, there are a whole lot of cool things for you to learn here, too!

WE CAN CHOOSE

COURAGE

OR WE CAN CHOOSE

COMFORT

BUT WE CAN'T

HAVE BOTH.

NOT AT THE

SAME TIME.

—BRENÉ BROWN

CHAPTER ONE
WHAT IS GROWTH MINDSET, ANYWAY?

We used to think the world was flat. We used to think animals didn't communicate with each other. We used to think there was no water on the moon. People have a lot of "used to's."

One big "used to" was thinking that the brain doesn't change, that it was a solid mass in your head that pretty much stayed the same your whole life. Well, thanks to **neuroscientists**, we now know that brains are **neuroplastic**—they stretch and grow just like you! Your brain is always growing because of the things you experience, think, feel, and do. That means your brain has limitless potential to learn.

In this first chapter, you'll see what learning has to do with a growth mindset. You'll get a crash course in "grit"—and how to harness it. Oh, yeah! And you'll uncover a magical, three-letter word that will open up your life.

Tapping into Your Superpower

You were born to learn. Before you even entered the world, you were listening to and experiencing the stimuli around you. Soon enough, your hunger to learn exploded! Your brain burst into incredible action. You gathered up information like squirrels gather nuts for the winter. You took in all sorts of new facts so that you could make sense of the world. Guess what? You continue to do this every day!

So, what does all of this knowledge collecting have to do with a growth mindset? What even is a growth mindset? **Growth**

mindset is the belief that your intelligence, abilities, skills, talents, and even personality are not fixed. These core aspects of who you are can change over time. How do they grow? They develop because of your ability to try, fail, and learn.

The most important part about growth mindset is the *belief* in your ability to learn. Learning is the key to everything! Humans' ability to learn gave us the cool discoveries and inventions we have so far. Without learning, you wouldn't have a phone, the clothes on your back, a refrigerator, or even this book!

Learning allows your intelligence to grow and expands the things you're good at. It makes you kinder to others and better able to understand how you and others may feel. Learning is limitless!

Think about that: You can actually cause your intelligence, abilities, skills, and talents to grow. You can get better and smarter at whatever you choose to focus on.

Growth Mindset versus Fixed Mindset

At about the same time that neuroscientist Marian Diamond was making her brain discoveries, another determined woman named Carol Dweck wanted to understand why some kids loved taking on challenges and others didn't. Carol grew up during a time when people thought the brain was a solid, unchangeable mass—that "smarts" were something you couldn't grow. She called this belief a "fixed mindset." Most people thought that whatever amount of intelligence you were born with was simply your share. They didn't know about **neuroplasticity**!

Carol knew something was off about that, so she set out to study it and discovered new answers. With curiosity and hard work, she discovered that what we believe about our intelligence makes a huge difference in what we achieve.

What else did Carol discover? She discovered that when you activate your growth mindset, you feel, think, and act in ways that make your brain grow. And guess what? When you activate your growth mindset, you gain really cool skills and talents, too.

Read the following chart to understand the difference between a growth mindset and one that is fixed.

MINDSET CHART

GROWTH MINDSET	FIXED MINDSET
Approach learning as a process to get better at something ("I don't know how to do that yet.")	Approach learning as an *event* to prove to others your smartness
Embrace challenges	Avoid challenges
View struggle as an opportunity to learn	Become easily frustrated and see frustration as a sign to give up
Seek advice	Seek praise rather than advice
View feedback as a way to improve	View feedback as a critique
Ask for help when learning something	Avoid asking for help because you fear others might think you don't know how to do something
Use a variety of learning techniques and strategies	Use minimal learning techniques and strategies
View mistakes and failures as opportunities to learn and grow	See mistakes and failure as a sign that you're not smart or capable

→

GROWTH MINDSET	FIXED MINDSET
Persevere in the face of setbacks and obstacles	Give up easily in the face of setbacks and obstacles
See effort and hard work as the path to learning	See effort and hard work as a waste of time
Feel inspired by the success of others	Feel threatened by the success of others

Adapted from Nigel Holmes' infographic and Carol Dweck's book *Mindset*.

If you find yourself relating to a lot of the fixed mindset habits, that's okay! We all do sometimes because there are many old fixed-mindset messages surrounding us. Sometimes it takes some unlearning to move ourselves from fixed mindset to growth mindset patterns. No matter how much you have to learn, you once knew less than you knew today, and you persevered through that. Congratulations!

List two things that you've learned. Pat yourself on the back for exercising your growth mindset!

What would you add? List two or three things you want to learn more about. Do any of these build on knowledge, skills, or talents you already have? Make a note about how learning new things relates to things you already know, think, feel, and do.

What's Grit?

There once was a girl who took a math class. She was focused and asked questions. She took notes. When she didn't get something the first time, she tried again and again. She struggled! But then she tried a different strategy. She discovered that she could learn from her mistakes, and she asked for more help.

This girl's teacher noticed her hard work and the way she used different ways to learn. She saw the young mathematician's ability to learn, to get better at the thing she focused on. The girl's focus and hard work paid off! The teacher was so inspired by her student's effort that she set out to learn about a four-letter word: **grit**.

The math teacher's name was Angela Duckworth. Angela's curiosity led her around the world, studying how people got better at the things they deeply cared about. Angela asked questions, took notes, struggled, tried different strategies, made and learned from mistakes, and asked for help. Angela did all the things she saw her math student doing. Angela was exercising her grit.

Let's see what this looks like when we try it. Imagine something you deeply care about. Maybe it's taking care of animals or programming your own computer. Maybe it's playing basketball or writing. Maybe it's singing music or starting your own business. It could be advocating on behalf of climate change or girls' education around the world!

I CARE ABOUT _____

_____

_____

Now imagine paying a lot of attention to what you wrote down, really focusing and spending time on it. You learn more about it, study it, practice it, talk about it, and share it with others. You take on new challenges that help you get better at it—and continue even when it's hard. You say "yes" to new experiences that involve your passion. *This* is grit.

How can you increase your grit? Try these steps.

1. First, ask yourself, "What am I interested in?" or "What do I want to get better at?"

----

2. Next, focus on the interest you identified. Write down two things you can do to learn more about it.

----

3. Then, take action! Write down two things you can do to take action tomorrow.

---

4. Finally, be patient and kind to yourself. Write down two things you will do to be extra kind to yourself.

Note: Know that your interests and passions may change as you get older. That's okay, too!

Passion and Perseverance

Angela defines grit as the combination of using **passion** and **perseverance** to work toward long-term goals. Let's unpack "passion" and "perseverance." Having "passion" for something means you deeply care about it. You value it and think it's really important. "Perseverance" means you commit to making this thing grow, even when obstacles or people get in your way! You might struggle or fail. You might experience something that distracts you. But you stick with it.

> "When you're knocked down, get right back up and never listen to anyone who says you can't or shouldn't go on."
>
> —HILLARY RODHAM CLINTON, LAWYER, FORMER FIRST LADY OF THE UNITED STATES, FORMER U.S. SENATOR, AND FORMER SECRETARY OF STATE

Does this sound tough? Sometimes it is hard to stick with things, even when we care about them. But grit is what gives us the power to see it through. Grit gets us to a place where we are happy and proud of all that we have learned and done. Grit makes us feel like we can learn anything!

How do you know if you have it? That's easy.

WE ALL HAVE GRIT.

How can you use it and make it grow? The more you exercise your grit, the more grit you'll get!

Having passion for something means you care about it deeply. Passion makes it easier and more fun to push through that gritty phase. So, what's "passion sauce"?

Passion sauce is like a recipe that allows you to combine ingredients to create something delicious. When you mix together the following ingredients in yourself, you create a passion sauce that makes your power grow. Your passion sauce is your ability to make things happen.

PASSION SAUCE RECIPE

ONE PART KNOWLEDGE ABOUT HOW YOUR BRAIN GROWS FROM LEARNING

ONE PART PASSION

ONE PART PERSISTENCE AND DEDICATION

ONE PART GROWTH MINDSET

A Magical Three-Letter Word: Yet!

You may not understand the magic of "yet" yet, but you soon will!

"Yet" is understanding how time and learning go together. You may not know how to do something right now, but that's because you haven't learned how to *yet*. You need time, experience, and probably a lot of mistakes and failures to truly learn something. Do you want to know a cool trick? Try putting "yet" at the end of any sentence about something you can't do.

I can't ride a bike yet.

I can't do algebra yet.

I can't draw yet.

When you add "yet" to a sentence, it turns the things that are difficult for you into things you can do. "Yet" is the magic word that helps you learn anything you want with a commitment to learning.

Getting better at something involves a formula—a magical formula you can access at any time. Ready? You get better at things when you decide to learn more about them. After you make this commitment to yourself, next comes the hard part of pushing through the uncomfortable stage when it's still new and difficult. Remember the girl in the math class? She had to try and fail, ask for help, be patient with herself, and persevere.

The combination of growth mindset ("I believe I can learn how to do this.") and grit ("I can work through the hard parts.") is how you get better at something. When you approach new things with this belief and attitude, you can get better at whatever you choose.

TRY THIS! MAKE A "YET" LIST

What are three things you can't do *yet*? Fill in the bubbles to add to your list of things you are about to learn.

The Stories We Tell Ourselves

Did you know that your brain is a natural storyteller? In fact, it's the oldest and wisest storyteller on the planet!

The brain writes stories to help you make sense of the world around you. Some are short—just a word or a sentence. Some are long, with paragraphs, and others are epic—chapters upon chapters! Your brain is constantly receiving information, organizing it, and putting it together in story form. You are editing, revising, and rewriting. You have a whole library of stories in your brain!

With all of this going on in your head, it is normal to tell yourself stories about what you are good at. The problem comes when you tell yourself stories about things you *think* you are not good at. (It's simply not true!) It's also a problem when you say you don't like something and connect that to not being able to do it.

There is a big difference between "I don't like public speaking" and "I'm not good at public speaking." When you say you don't like something, you're communicating a preference. We all have things we like or don't like, and that's totally normal. But when you state that you aren't good at something or can't do it, that becomes a **self-limiting story**. That's when you give up before you even start. If you decide you do like public speaking (or any other activity) and you want to learn it, a growth mindset story sounds like this: "I can't present in front of others *yet*" or "I know when I present I will feel nervous, but that's totally normal!"

Once you start to look at things you can't do *yet* as opportunities to try, experiment, better understand, and learn, your world will open up. Believe in what you will someday learn with time, focus, patience, and perseverance. Trust that it will take you to new places and make life more fun and exciting.

SHE GOT GRIT!

Imagine believing in the power of education so badly that you will do anything to make sure you and other girls can go to school. At age 15, Malala Yousafzai survived an attempted attack on her life that was intended to stop her from defending the right of girls to go to school in Pakistan. Malala didn't stop—and she still hasn't stopped. In 2014, she was awarded the Nobel Peace Prize, becoming the youngest person ever to receive the honor. That's what it looks like to never give up.

Checking In on Your Stories

Sometimes you tell yourself a story for so long that you start to believe it. It's healthy to check in with these stories every once in a while to see if they are still true. Let's say the story you tell yourself is "I can't play the piano." You might go your whole life not knowing how much fun it is to tickle the keys. You might miss the opportunity to join a band, play in front of crowds of people, and make new friends. You might even miss the chance to travel around the world playing music!

If you find yourself telling a story like this, see if you can reframe it: "I can't play the piano *yet*." When you commit to learning something new, you usually know it's going to be hard. (No one said playing the piano was easy!) But it's important to focus on all of the amazing opportunities that can come from believing in your abilities and putting in a little extra time and effort.

Try to change the story so that it makes sense to you, respects you, values you, and appreciates you. Your stories should expand your world, support you, challenge you, and empower you. Your stories should allow you to grow your power, potential, and possibilities.

Can you think of three limiting stories you might have told yourself? (This can be a vulnerable experience, so it's okay to skip it and come back later.) Now, flip the script! Rewrite each of the stories you listed while exercising your growth mindset. Remember: Adding "yet" can change our stories from limited to limitless!

LIMITING STORY	NEW STORY!

Which of these stories makes you feel powerful and brave? Is one story more fun? A cool thing about growth mindset is that it expands all of the amazing things we are capable of doing.

The Hard Work Story

One outdated or misunderstood story is that hard work is boring. Can you turn this old story into a fresh one?

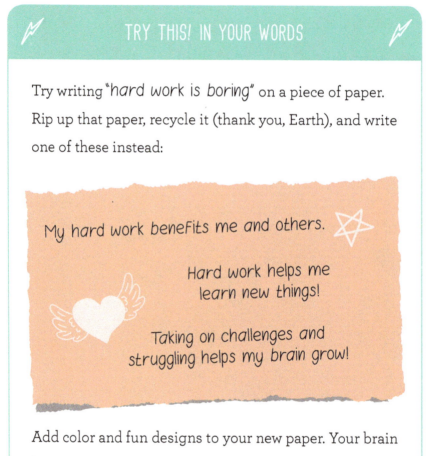

TRY THIS! IN YOUR WORDS

Try writing "*hard work is boring*" on a piece of paper. Rip up that paper, recycle it (thank you, Earth), and write one of these instead:

My hard work benefits me and others.

Hard work helps me learn new things!

Taking on challenges and struggling helps my brain grow!

Add color and fun designs to your new paper. Your brain loves pictures!

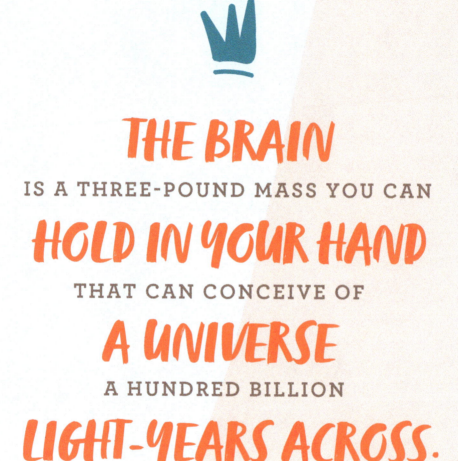

THE BRAIN
IS A THREE-POUND MASS YOU CAN
HOLD IN YOUR HAND
THAT CAN CONCEIVE OF
A UNIVERSE
A HUNDRED BILLION
LIGHT-YEARS ACROSS.

—MARIAN DIAMOND

CHAPTER TWO
YOUR STRETCHY BRAIN

Did you know that a growth mindset relates directly to your brain? That's right! When you try new things, make mistakes, and learn, learn, learn—your brain changes with you. Learning more about how the brain operates helps you understand how a growth mindset works to make your life bigger, better, and more daring.

A Look at Your Brain

Our brain is the most powerful learning ecosystem on the planet. Why? Because its potential is limitless. The more you stretch it, the stronger it gets. Your stretchy brain, in this very moment, has limitless ability to create something new.

Like us, neuroscientists are always learning. They are taking risks, exposing themselves to new challenges, and learning from mistakes. They are trying out new approaches and learning new things about the brain all the time. They are making their brains stronger and smarter by studying how the brain grows stronger and smarter—just like you!

How Does the Brain Work?

Your brain is made up of several key parts that work together to experience the world around you. Your brain is working when you sit, see, run, think, feel—even sleep!

There are many parts of the brain that neuroscientists are learning more and more about. Let's have a closer look.

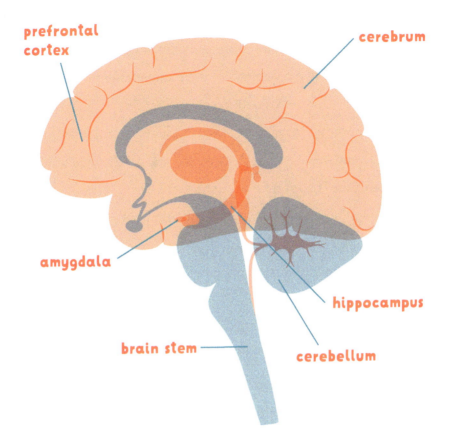

prefrontal
cortex

cerebrum

amygdala

hippocampus

brain stem

cerebellum

Are you sitting and reading this guide? You're able to because your **cerebellum** helps you keep your balance and coordinates all your movements, from sitting and standing to walking, running, and writing.

What do you see? What do you hear? If you can answer those questions, thank your **cerebrum**. Your cerebrum supports your core senses and your thinking, your talking, the processing of your emotions, and your learning.

Breathing in . . . breathing out, and other automatic things our bodies do? These come from your **brain stem**. It connects your cerebellum and cerebrum to your spinal cord so you can do the things your body needs to do automatically, like breathe, pump your heart, digest food, swallow, sleep, sneeze, and cough.

Want to remember what you've read so far? Engage your **hippocampus**. It supports your short-term and long-term memories. It also helps with learning and processing your emotions.

What happened the last time you felt scared? Did you fight, flee, freeze, or faint? These are the various responses that we (and animals!) use to respond to threatening situations. You can thank your **amygdala** for your ability to respond to danger. Survival is extremely important, and that's why the amygdala has gotten so much attention for keeping us alive. But we are also learning that the amygdala plays a key role in supporting other emotions and our memory.

What about the part that regulates choices, decisions, planning, and self-control? It's because of the **prefrontal cortex** that you can decide what to eat for a snack, what time to go to sleep, and how to use this book. This part of the brain is key to applying a growth mindset, since it's what helps you step out of your comfort zone in a healthy way. With the prefrontal cortex on your side, you can take on that challenge today, tomorrow, or anytime you put your mind to it!

That's a lot of brain science. Let's pause (thank you, prefrontal cortex). Adjust your sitting position (thank you, cerebellum). Take a slow, deep breath, in through your nose, 1-2-3, and out through your mouth, 1-2-3 (thank you, brain stem). One more: Breathe in, 1-2-3, and breathe out, 1-2-3. Breathing like this regulates your mind and body, changing the chemistry of your brain.

Growing a Stronger Brain

Your brain grows neurons at an insane rate—so fast that neuro-scientists can't keep up with how many neurons per second the brains grow! **Neurons** are the brain's main growing material. But what do neurons do? And how does neuroplasticity work?

The brain is made up of a network of neurons.

Neurons communicate with each other through electrical and chemical processes.

When we learn something, the brain grows in various ways.

New neurons grow. This is called **neurogenesis**.

Neurons connect to form new pathways.

Those new pathways connect.

Existing pathways get stronger and expand into networks.

The more we use our brains, the more neurons, connections, and stronger neural pathways we cause to grow. What's the recipe for a stronger brain?

* Step out of your comfort zone.

* Take on a new challenge—and stick with it!

* Put forth effort and practice something.

* Make and learn from your mistakes.

* Take learning risks!

One of the best things you can do to make your brain grow is to make mistakes. Your brain loves mistakes so much, it actually lights up when you make them. When you make what your brain perceives to be a mistake, your brain literally becomes more active. It acts like it's playing a game!

Hey, I Remember That!

Think about the number of things you've learned over your entire life. Thousands? Millions? Billions? Can you even count that high? The interesting thing is, you probably don't remember how hard each new thing was when you first started, because over time, it became natural.

Everything starts out hard. But when we dedicate attention, energy, and effort, it becomes easier.

Elephants are known for their great memory.

(PAST) Can you remember two things you've learned in the past?

_____

_____

_____

(PRESENT) What are some things you are learning right now? List two.

_____

_____

_____

(FUTURE) What do you want to learn and dedicate your time to next? List one thing you will start to learn this week.

_____

_____

_____

_____

Creativity and the Brain

As we get older, our creativity grows, too. You may have noticed how something that you wrote, drew, or created when you were younger isn't quite what you'd write, draw, or create now. Try not to be too hard on your young self! You were learning how to hold a pencil while directing it to draw the picture in your mind. Your work was causing a neural pathway to grow. Appreciate your young self's time, energy, effort, mistakes, and struggle! This work is the very reason you're able to write, draw, and create what you can today.

The thing is, this process doesn't just apply to writing or drawing. We have the ability to think creatively about everything, from how to garden to how to give a speech. A growth mindset helps us look at old problems in new ways.

> "Don't let anyone rob you of your imagination, your creativity, or your curiosity. It's your place in the world; it's your life. Go on and do all you can with it, and make it the life you want to live."
>
> —MAE JEMISON, THE FIRST AFRICAN AMERICAN WOMAN ASTRONAUT IN SPACE

Thinking Big

As we get older, we understand that there are different types of thinking. When we think more creatively about big ideas, this is called **abstract thinking**. Abstract thinking allows us to step back and think about a problem in a bigger way. We often compare abstract thinking to **concrete thinking**. For example, if you think about one puppy, you are thinking concretely about a single object. If you think about puppies in general (and how much you love them), you are thinking abstractly about our furry friends.

Abstract thinking applies to our thoughts, emotions, actions, and interactions, too. What might this look like? You know all the times your younger sibling or friends bug you—maybe they mess with your stuff? If you think concretely about the person, you might get frustrated. But if you think about your friendship or loving relationship abstractly, it might encourage you to give the person a break.

Seeing the big picture can help us communicate in more creative and helpful ways. You can put yourself in their shoes—this is called **empathy**. Your growth mindset activates your curiosity about their life and the experiences you share.

"Why" questions always follow a good dose of curiosity. "Why are they always wanting to play with me or come into my room or mess with my stuff?" The answer could be "Oh, they care about and love me! They look up to me, so of course they always want to be around me." This way of thinking can give you a deeper look at their motivations, which can help you be understanding and respond in ways that make everyone feel better.

TRY THIS! PRACTICING EMPATHY

Can you think of a time when someone did something annoying? List that in Column A on the left. Now, think about *why* that person might have done that— what they might be going through or what they might have wanted. See if you can think abstractly about that person. Write down the "big picture"—what might be happening in their world—in Column B on the right.

COLUMN A: THAT BUGGED ME	COLUMN B: BIG PICTURE

Creative Outlets

Your brain loves to create. The great news? New and exciting opportunities are all around you! Give your brain what it craves. Remember: Creative outlets come in many forms.

How do you channel your creativity? Start by paying attention to the world around you. Write down two things you notice going on around you.

_____

_____

_____

_____

_____

Be curious. Write down one question you have today.

_____

_____

_____

_____

Saying "Yes"!

Saying "yes" sometimes feels scary because the amygdala is trying to do its thing to protect you from danger. The thing is, the amygdala doesn't always realize the difference between something that is actually dangerous (like standing on the edge of a cliff) and something that is a learning opportunity (like signing up for an art class) until it gets more information.

Get more information by learning more details about the opportunity. When is it happening? How long is the commitment? When you say, "Yes, I will check it out," know that you can always change your mind after you learn more about it. Then, bring that healthy fear along for the ride!

TRY THIS! MAPPING WORDS TO EMOTIONS

I am excited to say "yes" to

When I think about learning it, I feel

Something else I am thinking about saying "yes" to

When I think about learning this, I feel

What do you need in order to say "yes" to this opportunity?

IF YOUR

DREAMS

DO NOT

SCARE YOU,

THEY ARE NOT

BIG ENOUGH.

—ELLEN JOHNSON SIRLEAF

CHAPTER THREE
YOUR POWERFUL MIND

Your brain and mind both grow, expand, and hold limitless power, potential, and possibilities. But what's the relationship between the two? How do they work together?

There are lots of common phrases that have to do with the mind. Maybe you've heard some of them.

"I changed my mind."

"Keep an open mind."

"What's on your mind?"

These sentences have the "mind" in common. But what do they mean? Why do we say "I changed my mind" instead of "I changed my brain"? In this chapter, you'll see what the brain and mind have in common and how they work together to help you learn, calm down in times of stress, and explore the world.

A Closer Look at the Mind

Your brain is an ever-changing system that resides in your head. It is a physical, tangible thing. But what is the mind?

Loosely put, your mind is your inside world. When you stop to take a moment to look at your inside world, you end up focusing on your breath and your body. In these moments, you might also start to notice the world around you. You slow things down and form a new relationship to your thoughts.

This slowing down of the mind makes your brain an even more powerful tool. How? It gives you a chance to look more closely at your thoughts, fears, and dreams without judging them. One tool you have to observe your thoughts is known as mindfulness.

What Is Mindfulness?

Mindfulness is when you are aware of what is going on in the present moment. Right . . . now! The trick is trying not to change the thoughts you are having—just to look at them. Can you look at your thoughts as if they were clouds floating by? When you look at your thought like a cloud, you don't try to change it. You simply see it for what it is.

Mindfulness gives you the power to pay attention to what you want. Your mind believes everything you tell it, so remember to feed it the healthy stuff and recycle or toss out whatever is unhealthy!

Write down three healthy things you are going to do to feed your mind.

1. _____

   _____

2. _____

   _____

3. _____

   _____

If you've heard of mindfulness, you might also have heard of meditating. You might even imagine people sitting on the ground or a pillow, legs crossed, peacefully watching their thoughts go by. You'd be spot-on! Mindfulness and meditation are related. **Meditation** is the practice of tuning in to your inside world—your thoughts, emotions, and bodily sensations. It's not about trying to turn off these thoughts but rather saying "hello" to them without trying to make them disappear. While sitting on a comfy pillow is one way to meditate, there are also many other ways. Meditation is more about how you relate to your thoughts than how you sit or where you are.

Sit comfortably. Close your eyes or gently lower your gaze to the floor. Slowly breathe in, 1-2-3, and breathe out, 1-2-3. Again: Breathe in, 1-2-3; breathe out, 1-2-3.

Think about your body. Start with the bottoms of your feet; then move up your legs to your knees, thighs, belly. Move to your hands, elbows, shoulders. To your chest, neck. To your face and then the top of your head. You are transported into your mind, to your inside world.

Imagine your favorite place of warmth and calm. What does it look and smell like? What does your body feel like when you're there? Walk toward this place and plop down. Stay as long as you'd like. Now imagine a fluffy cloud of softness, warmth, and calm surrounding you. Feel relief washing over you. You feel safe, respected, appreciated. You are valued, supported, confident, relaxed.

Look around and hear, "Welcome back." Breathe in, 1-2-3, and breathe out, 1-2-3. Return to this place anytime. Just close your eyes.

Catching Your Thoughts

What are you thinking? No, really—what are you thinking right now? Can you catch it? Sometimes your thoughts are hard to catch because they are moving quickly and you're having so many of them all the time. They blow in and out 24/7 like those clouds across our "mind sky." Sometimes your mind sky is full of dark storm clouds. Other times it's painted with fluffy white clouds, hazy clouds, or other types of clouds.

It can be challenging to hear and catch your fast-moving thoughts. Your inside world can be a busy place! You are thinking, feeling, processing, remembering, experiencing the world around you, having opinions, and learning. You are aware of some thoughts, and you are not aware of others (that's your subconscious). The following tool can help you slow your thoughts down enough to catch them.

The key is to pause long enough to look into your mind sky to catch them. Let's practice pausing for a few moments. Put the book down, tune in to your mind, and hear your thoughts. Ready? PAUSE.

Welcome back. How did it go? Were you able to catch any thoughts? Take a moment to write down a few of them.

When you do this, you get to know yourself better. And, after all, you're the most important person to know and understand and love.

As you get better at practicing mindfulness, you can practice it throughout the day, whether you're reading, sitting, walking, eating, playing basketball, listening to music, designing, creating, solving a math problem, painting, drawing, or listening to a friend. At any point in your day, you can practice pausing by scheduling time to check in with yourself.

1. Find a comfortable spot and tune in to your body, your physical presence. Become aware of what you are doing. Right now, for example, you are sitting and reading these words.

2. Slow down your movements. Since you are reading right now, you are in a ready state to S-L-O-W D-O-W-N. Can you be even more still?

3. Mentally press a pause button. Let all the activity of your life melt away for the moment.

4. See if you can turn down the noise of the world around you. This allows you to pay attention to your breath.

5. Finally, tune in to your inside world. Hear your thoughts, blowing in and out like clouds in your mind sky.

Sticky Thoughts

Learning how to learn is extremely important. But so is learning how to *un*learn! With this guide, you are practicing how to say "hello" to new experiences and opportunities and how to say "goodbye" to old, outdated, and often hurtful ways of thinking.

During this process, sometimes a certain thought stays around longer than you'd like. It gets stuck on repeat. This is called **ruminating**. Why is a particular thought on repeat? Because whatever you pay attention to *grows* in your mind and brain.

This is great news! It means that when we are mindful about our thoughts, we can grow the ones that make us thrive.

Supportive Self-Talk

All day long, you have conversations with yourself. Sometimes you are aware of these conversations, and other times, you are not. These conversations are totally normal! Everyone has them.

We call these conversations **self-talk**. While sometimes your self-talk can feel like chatter, these conversations with yourself can help you tap deeply into your power and potential.

Remember our guidelines for writing, editing, and revising the stories we tell ourselves? You can use these same guidelines to know whether your self-talk is:

* Respecting you
* Appreciating you
* Supporting you
* Challenging you
* Empowering you

If you find your mind wandering to a place that doesn't make you feel good, remember that is normal. As best you can, try to respect that space and know that feeling is temporary. After you've given that thought enough room and feel ready to move on, know that you can change the channel.

Read each thought and decide whether it is supportive, helpful, and kind. Does it meet our guidelines? Revise those that need some changes.

THOUGHT	SUPPORTIVE? HELPFUL? KIND?	REVISED THOUGHT
I was really kind to myself today.	Yes Not yet	
I need to quickly hide that mistake so someone doesn't see it.	Yes Not yet	
I smiled at the new student today.	Yes Not yet	
I started a new project, and I'm really excited about it.	Yes Not yet	
I failed my test because I'm not good at math.	Yes Not yet	

Mindful Writing

Writing is another powerful mindfulness practice. It's a way to catch your thoughts and emotions. When you write, you slow down your mind. You can take what you are experiencing in your inside world and bring it to your outside world. Writing brings the two worlds together.

Pen and paper exist in the outside world. Your thoughts and emotions exist in your inside world.

One way to explore your thoughts and emotions is through journaling. Journaling is a judgment-free space to explore what's going on inside your mind and heart. It has a really special audience of one: You!

How do you get started with journaling?

1. Get a pen and paper. You can use the space below or grab a journal!

2. To start a new habit, choose a specific time of day to journal.

3. Write about whatever you want. Try to put your thoughts and emotions into words or pictures or doodles.

4. It's totally normal for lots of thoughts to fly into your mind sky. Acknowledge them. Then practice blowing them back out and choosing the ones you want to focus on by writing them down.

5. Be free. Be curious.

Here are some prompts to get you started:

* When you think about your brain and mind growing, what image do you see?

* What was the coolest mistake you made today?

* What new challenge do you want to take on?

* What new skill are you proud of?

→

It's Okay to Unplug

It's okay to put the stick down. (Huh?)

At one point, sticks were our technology, and we carried them around with us like we carry our phones today. We used to love to figure out ways to use our sticks to help us make something easier and more efficient. We wanted to use our sticks to create, to build. Sticks were our tools. We rubbed them together to make fire, and then we figured out ways to use the fire we created with our tools.

Throughout the day in caves around the neighborhood, you could hear early human parents telling their kids, "Put your stick away! It's time to eat," or "Put your stick away! It's time to sleep." And early human kids responded with "Yeah, but I am playing with my stick!" And early human parents would say back, "But it's taking away from you being connected with others because you're only focused on your stick." Maybe they didn't say it quite like that, but you get the picture.

Sticks were super fun and a powerful learning tool. It is also important to remember that when those early kids put down their sticks, it gave them room to think about new ideas. Early kids eventually learned to put their technology down to open themselves up to new ideas and inventions.

When you put your "stick" down and tune in to what's happening around you, you can spend more time exploring and creating.

From Belly to Bed

Your body needs to eat, sleep, and play, and so do your brain and mind. Eating is your time to fuel your body, brain, and mind. Eating nutritious food gives you the energy and vitamins you need to operate at your full capacity. Mealtime is also a great time to practice mindfulness because you can engage all of your core senses.

Next time you sit down to eat a snack, try to notice these sensations. What does the food smell like? Taste like? How does it feel when you chew and swallow? Can you imagine where it was grown or how it was produced? See if you can notice something new about your snack. Can you count the number of times you chew?

Sleep is also so important to your overall health because it's the longest period of time in the 24-hour cycle when your body, brain, and mind rest! Many people use their bedtime routine to slow down and practice gratitude. Some people engage in mindful breathing to prepare their body, brain, and mind for rest. Do you have a bedtime routine?

For the next few nights, see if you can create a new bedtime routine for yourself. What do you do one hour before bed? How about 30 minutes? What do you think right before you fall asleep? Write these down before bed. The next morning, see how you feel and jot down some notes. Do you notice any patterns?

BEFORE BED: ONE HOUR

→

BEFORE BED: 30 MINUTES

BEFORE BED: TWO MINUTES

NEXT MORNING

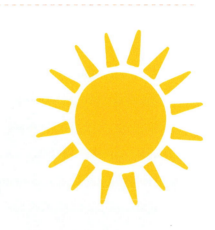

THE VERY ACT OF

DOING
THE THING

THAT SCARED ME

UNDID
THE FEAR.

—SHONDA RHIMES

CHAPTER FOUR

TAKE FEAR ALONG FOR THE RIDE

Now that you understand more about the brain and how to settle the mind, we'll take a look at something that seems like growth mindset's enemy but is actually its friend. I'm talking about Fear.

Fear is a fascinating emotion that has kept us alive for a long time—a very long time. Thank you, Fear! We appreciate you. While Fear can be our friend, we also need to keep it in check because sometimes it takes its job to protect us too seriously. When this happens, we end up missing out on opportunities to be challenged and inspired!

In this chapter, you will explore how to embrace fear as it moves its way through different learning and growth zones—at home, at school, and in your future. We'll also see what these zones have to do with mistakes and curiosity.

Understanding the Basic Zones

There are different "zones" that you enter whenever you participate in an activity. You might have heard of some of them before. You have a **comfort zone**, a **fear zone**, a **learning zone**, and a **growth zone**. In each zone, you think, feel, and experience different things. Everyone's zones are unique to them, so your fear zone might be different than a friend's fear zone.

What do your zones look and feel like?

Comfort Zone: You feel safe and in control.

Fear Zone: Fear makes itself known. It alerts you, and you start to figure out ways to avoid the thing that's causing you to feel scared or anxious.

Learning Zone: You may feel nervous or anxious or frustrated, curious or calm or excited or proud. You try new things, take risks, practice, make mistakes, fail, and gain new knowledge and skills.

Growth Zone: You may feel scared or nervous or anxious or frustrated, curious or calm or excited or proud. We use what we learn, we set goals, and we take some type of action to move forward.

There are lots of ways to move through these zones. The important thing is to start paying attention to how you feel after you make a decision or take on a challenge. When you look closer at how you make decisions, you'll learn more about yourself and your zones.

Fear and Growth Decisions

We make decisions all day long—hundreds of them, maybe even thousands. Some are simple, and some are complicated.

Some we are aware of, and some we are not. One thing that's for sure is that decisions usually fall into one of two categories: There are **fear-based decisions** and **growth-based decisions**.

Fear-based decisions are made because Fear wants to have its way and keep us from danger. Fear aims to keep us in our comfort and fear zones and away from our learning and growth zones. Fear means well, but it holds us back.

Growth-based decisions are made when we're able to let Fear know we are not in danger. We must acknowledge Fear's warning to keep us safe and then bring Fear along for the ride—even when Fear may be screaming out the window.

Keep in mind: Other emotions, like Joy and Pride, step up when you make growth-based decisions. Once you get going, Fear quiets down and enjoys the journey.

Here are just a few examples of fear-based versus growth-based decisions:

FEAR-BASED DECISIONS	GROWTH-BASED DECISIONS
You say "no" when someone asks you to share your work in a public place (a presentation, for example) because you fear what others may think about you.	You say "yes" when someone asks you to share your work in a public place because you know that "yes" helps your confidence and courage expand.
You say "no" to a challenge because you fear making mistakes or failing.	You say "yes" to a challenge because you know that challenges make your brain and mind stronger and smarter—mistakes do, too!
You decide to take the easier math class because you want to be able to get all of the answers right.	You push yourself to take the harder math class, get help from a tutor, and learn so much more!

Now it's your turn. Can you continue adding to each side of the following list?

→

FEAR-BASED DECISIONS	GROWTH-BASED DECISIONS

When you start to pay closer attention to when you make a decision out of fear and when you make one out of growth, you'll start to see yourself growing in new, unexpected, and challenging (and also super fun) ways.

What If

When we're about to step out of our comfort and fear zones and into our learning and growth zones, we sometimes stumble down a "what if" rabbit hole. We start to think about all the things that can go wrong.

Here are just a few you might recognize:

* What if I forget the words during my presentation?

* What if I fall down on the stage during my performance?

* What if they laugh at me?

* What if my ears go numb and my tongue swells and I can't even talk or hear them laughing at me and when I try to run away, I trip and fall and stumble down the rabbit hole of "what ifs"? I mean, it *could* happen!

"What if" thinking is totally normal. It gives us the pause we might need to double-check with ourselves that we are safe. It also might give us what we need in the moment to move forward. How? Because more often than not, our "what ifs" are far from the truth and rarely happen. It can even be quite fascinating to see what creative "what if" scenarios our imaginations can come up with.

See if you can notice a "what if" rabbit hole the next time you make a decision. Can you catch yourself, take the power away from the scary "what if," and make a growth decision?

SAFETY NOTE: "What if" thoughts can give you a moment of pause to check in with your gut. Listen to your gut instinct. If you are in physical or emotional danger and do not feel safe, please talk with a trusted adult as soon as possible.

An Unlikely Sidekick: Mistakes!

On the journey of life, you will meet many obstacles—maybe even a few villains. You'll get knocked down and then get up—only to repeat the process. You'll also have many successes and adventures to celebrate! Along the way, do you know who one of your most loyal sidekicks will be? Mistakes!

With a growth mindset, you'll find yourself taking on bigger and more fun challenges. With bigger challenges, you'll make more mistakes. And guess what? That's the goal! But what do we mean by mistakes, and how can we start to look at mistakes as part of our exciting journey?

At some point, the word "mistake" came to mean something to avoid. We started using it to describe things we believed to be wrong or incorrect. We then started to describe a collection of mistakes as a failure. But when we learn from our mistakes, does failure exist? (The answer is NO!) Mistakes spark our learning and fire up our brain.

A team of neuroscientists and psychologists found that when you make a mistake, synapses fire in your brain. The brain sparks and grows when you make a mistake, even if you are not aware of it. Because of the struggle, the brain grows!

There is so much to learn, unlearn, or relearn about and from mistakes. For example, not all mistakes are created equal. Some mistakes have bigger consequences than others. The most important question is not "How big was your mistake?" The question we care most about is "What did you learn, unlearn, or relearn from your mistake?"

TRY THIS! REWRITING MISTAKES

At some point, a sad story got passed around that said, "Mistakes and failures are bad." This is a good one to rip up and throw out or revise. Write *"mistakes are bad"* on a slip of paper—then tear it up and throw it away! On a fresh piece of paper, write:

Making mistakes makes my brain grow!

Add some fun details, pictures, symbols, or emojis.

Learning from Mistakes

Is there a time when we want to reduce mistakes and bring all our effort and practice together for a performance, a game, or a presentation? Absolutely. We want to minimize mistakes during these times. But even then, failures and losses happen, and that's totally normal.

Many of the world's inventions and discoveries came about because of mistakes and failures—from the lightbulb to chocolate chip cookies to Play-Doh. Someone was trying to make something, take on a challenge, or solve a problem, and they ended up discovering or creating something new along the way. *Trying* is the key word here. During the *trying* process, they made mistakes, and out of those mistakes, a new invention was born.

When you're in your learning and growth zones, it's much easier to welcome mistakes. Practice saying, "Hi, Mistake! It's nice to see you again. You showing up means I am learning."

We know that mistakes are normal because we're learning— we're trying something new. In this mindset, we understand that mistakes have to happen. The learning and growth zones are mistake-making and mistake-taking zones.

Key mis-TAKE-aways for you:

* Mistakes cause your brain to spark and grow.

* Mistakes give you information.

* Mistakes help you learn and grow.

* Not all mistakes are created equal.

* Making and learning from mistakes causes your power, potential, and possibilities to expand.

Getting to Know Your Mistakes

Mistakes are extremely valuable: Mistakes give us information that will help us. Every mistake we make is an opportunity to learn, unlearn, or relearn something. Greet mistakes with friendliness and curiosity, just like we greet our thoughts and emotions.

You can even try talking to your mistakes. Ask, "Mistake, what are you here to teach me?" Then listen. Listen closely. Approach your mistake like you're an investigator. Get as much information as you can from it. Then use the information you gain for your next try. We love do-overs, try-agains, and re-dos. That's what learning is all about.

Can you think of any mistakes you made that helped you when you tried again? How did it go? Write down a few recent mistakes you made and what you learned from each one.

MISTAKE	HOW IT HELPED ME

A Place Where Mistakes Hide

Sometimes school feels like a place where mistakes and failing are not welcome. Sometimes it feels like a place where people are constantly being judged and evaluated, and so you might feel like you need to know the right answers all the time. You might even feel like you can't ask questions or say, "I don't know yet." We call a place like this, where mistakes and failing are not welcomed, a **performance zone**.

This is a big problem because school is a place for learning and growth. Mistakes and failing automatically happen when we're learning! When we're busy being worried about making mistakes and failing, we stay in our comfort and fear zones and do not maximize our ability to learn, improve, and grow. Instead we are busy perfecting and proving to others that we have it all figured out—that we know the answers already.

You may have experienced these feelings about mistakes and failures at school. If you have, I am sorry. We adults need to do better to make school a safer place for learning—a place where risk-taking is encouraged and mistakes are celebrated! We need schools to be learning and growth zones.

What's exciting is that you are a member of the next generation that can transform both schools and learning outside schools. One way to get started? Share what you've learned about growth mindset with everyone you know!

THEY GOT GRIT!

You may or may not have started your period yet. But did you know there is a whole network of girls and women around the world advocating on your behalf? They want to help you celebrate your monthly menstrual cycle in a safe, healthy, supportive, and judgment-free space.

To help, girls just like you founded an organization called PERIOD in 2014. PERIOD and other organizations like HelloFlo aim to provide free, clean, and healthy period products in schools, shelters, and prisons.

Girls in these orgs educate others to change the way people think, talk, and learn about periods. They fight for system-wide change toward menstrual equality! They even organized the world's first #NationalPeriodDay on October 19, 2019, raising awareness around period poverty. Women and girls like you demanded that period products be more accessible and the tampon tax be eliminated once and for all.

There are many ways you can step into learning and growth zones at school. Here are just a few:

* Ask your friends at school to join you on your sports team.

* Invite someone you don't know yet to come with you to a new after-school club.

* Raise your hand in class. (And keep raising your hand even when you're not called on!)

* Share your thoughts and opinions inside and outside the classroom.

* Act on behalf of what you believe is important.

* Try something new!

What are other ways to step into a learning and growth zone at school? List two.

- -

- -

- -

- -

Growing at Home

Here are a few other ways to stretch yourself at home:

* Problem-solve with siblings, parents, grandparents, neighbors, and friends.

* Make new friends in your neighborhood.

* Sign up for a new class—art, boxing, dancing, music, whatever you like!

* Play a sport—basketball, soccer, swimming, lacrosse, archery, the choice is yours!

* Design or create something.

Have you ever wondered what mistakes and failures the adults in your life have made? Let's ask them. The following questions may help you understand a grown-up's experience with mistakes and what they have learned from them.

Pro tip: For best results, let adults know that you want to better understand them. Explain to them that you are trying to learn the meaning of a "mistake" and how they have worked through their own. Then, ask them any one of these questions. Better yet—make up your own!

* What does "mistake" mean to you?

* What does "failure" mean to you?

* What are some of your favorite mistakes?

* What are some of your favorite failures?

* Why did a particular mistake happen?

* Why did a particular failure happen?

* How did you feel when you made the mistake?

* How did you feel when you failed?

* What did you learn from your mistake?

* What did you learn from your failure?

Feel free to use the following pages to record some of their responses. The goal is for you to share a bonding experience with an adult you trust, learn from one another, and be curious about each other's lives.

THERE IS

NO
POETRY

WHERE THERE ARE

NO
MISTAKES.

—JOY HARJO

CHAPTER FIVE
NOBODY IS PERFECT

One of the main obstacles on the growth mindset journey is the desire to be perfect. But here's a secret: The idea of being perfect is just that—an idea. And this idea gets in your way!

When your goal is to be "perfect," you focus on proving to others that you are. But perfect is a made-up place. When you focus on being "perfect" in someone else's eyes, you miss out on your own journey—and the adventures that come with it!

Here we bust the myth of perfection and show how much more we see and grow when we make mistakes and try again.

So Much Is Waiting for You

Sometimes people avoid trying something new or hard because they may not be "perfect" at it. But think of all of the fun and amazing things you will miss out on if you don't even try! Here are just a few:

* Learning to play the guitar and traveling the world with a band

* Studying marine biology and swimming in the ocean with dolphins

* Learning another language and making friends from around the world

* Volunteering at an animal shelter and bringing care and comfort to a lost or wounded animal

There is so much out there, waiting for you. Let's explore how to avoid getting trapped in the quest for perfection and comparing yourselves to others. Instead, you'll learn how to better celebrate and support others—and yourself!

Perfection = A Performance

When there's no effort, struggle, or mistakes when you're learning, you're actually not learning. You're doing something, but you're not learning. You know how to get dressed and eat breakfast already, so you're just doing it.

Sometimes you stay focused on doing things you already know how to do because you're trying to prove to others that you're smart. They've sent you the message that they are evaluating and judging you, so you start showing them all the things you're good at. You start performing and proving, and soon you're stuck in a trap of "perfecting." Other times, the idea of failing takes over and we stop ourselves.

But learning is a process that involves effort, struggle, mistakes, and failure. Everything we learn starts out difficult at first—that's how you know you are stretching your brain. When something is easy, that means you already know how.

Let's explore what "perfect" means to you. Write down what "perfect" means to you in this moment:

Now, let's explore this definition. What happens when you understand that perfection is only an idea? Even cooler, what happens when the definition is up to you? In this exercise, you can change the word "perfect" to mean whatever you want. If "perfect" means to you that you just made a fun mistake because you tried something new, then that's what it means! In this way, "perfect" is what *you* want it to be, not what someone else wants it to be for you.

List three or four activities and come up with new definitions of "perfect" for those activities. If you write down "playing guitar," maybe the new definition of perfect is "playing a new song with lots of mistakes." Don't be afraid to come up with something wild and crazy! This is your game and your vision of perfection.

ACTIVITY	NEW "PERFECT"

Dust Yourself Off and Try Again

"Fall down seven times, get up eight."

"Get back on the horse that bucked you."

"The bamboo that bends is stronger than the oak that resists."

What do you think these idioms and proverbs mean?

Many expressions may not make sense logically when you actually break them apart, but as a whole, they still communicate a message. For example, when we dissect "Fall down seven times, get up eight," it doesn't make sense—if you fall down seven times, you actually get up seven times, not eight. So, what is the message?

When a setback or obstacle comes your way—and it will—stick with it and exercise your resiliency. Get back up. Bounce back. Keep going, even when it seems impossible.

I AM RESILIENT

SHE GOT GRIT!

When Serena Williams, tennis champion and one of the greatest athletes of all time, discovered the power of losing, she took her sport and her life to a new level.

"Sometimes you don't know how to be better if you are always doing it right," she said. "But if you fail, then you fall, and then you can rise up higher than you ever would have if you didn't fail."

Serena experienced a lot of "wins" in tennis, but she worked hard to get there. When pressure got in her way, she lost three Grand Slam tournaments in a row. She realized that in chasing perfection, she was getting in her own way.

She shifted her mindset, relaxed, and began to enjoy the game—her wins and losses. Then she won four Grand Slam tournaments in a row.

Feedback Is Your Friend

What do we mean by feedback? And where does it come from? **Feedback** is information you get from the outside world that helps move you forward. Feedback is your friend, and your friends give you feedback.

A couple of things to keep in mind:

* Not all feedback is pleasant to hear.

* Ask for feedback from trusted adults, peers, and friends.

* Not all feedback is created equal.

* DO NOT accept feedback that is a put-down.

Use your guidelines again. Does the feedback:

* Respect you?

* Appreciate you?

* Value you?

* Help you?

* Support you?

* Challenge you?

* Empower you?

* Expand your learning?

* Expand your power, potential, and possibilities?

Dr. Brené Brown offers us some advice about feedback: "A lot of cheap seats in the arena are filled with people who never venture onto the floor. They just hurl mean-spirited criticisms and put-downs from a safe distance."

She goes on to say that if someone is criticizing just to criticize or being mean or insulting, she doesn't accept that feedback. She lets it drop on the ground and leaves it there. This is advice we all can follow.

Life as a Curious Cat

Believe it or not, curiosity used to be something that made people afraid. Why? There was a time when curiosity was discouraged because certain (fixed-mindset) people wanted the world to stay exactly as it was. They didn't want people believing in themselves and asking questions about the way the world *could* be. People thought curiosity was to be controlled.

We know better now. Your curiosity is a magical tool that can take you around the world! Curiosity moves you forward and makes the world a better place. Curiosity is the seed that makes learning grow.

Curiosity is also the **antidote** to perfection. When we are curious about something, we just want to learn more about it, to try it out. We don't care how we perform or whether we get it right.

Ask yourself regularly:

* How can I stretch myself today?

* What am I curious about?

* What do I want to learn?

- -

- -

- -

A New Trick

Curiosity leads you to new challenges and adventures. But oftentimes, these adventures land you smack-dab in the middle of your fear zone! To manage this fear zone and keep going, you can use a few tricks. One of them is creating a **mantra**.

Mantras are statements that we repeat to draw our focus to a specific thought, intention, or aspect of ourselves. As you've already learned, the thoughts you pay attention to are the ones that grow. Instead of getting lost in your constantly moving thoughts, use a mantra to help you focus on a simple statement.

Here are a few mantras for you to try out, especially when you want to tap into a little extra courage.

* "I want my voice to be heard."

* "I want to be seen and heard."

* "I am courageous."

* "I am brave."

* "Where I am, so is courage."

* "Courage makes courage grow."

* "I am power."

* "I am unlimited potential."

As you start to practice your courage mantras, you'll likely tweak them to make them your own. Fill in the bubbles with your own courage mantras, but also feel free to stick to the ones listed!

SHE GOT GRIT!

When Hillary Rodham Clinton was a girl, she wanted to be an astronaut, not president of the United States. But she lived during a time when people didn't think women could or should be astronauts or president of the United States. (This was the case even though women were behind the scenes writing the math equations that sent astronauts into space!)

In 2008, Hillary Clinton ran for president and lost. But her failure didn't stop her—she went on to serve as secretary of state for President Obama, the candidate she had lost to that year. In 2016, she ran for president again—as the first woman to be nominated by a major political party. But she lost again. She tried twice and lost twice.

Since then, she has spent her time inspiring and supporting girls and women all over the world, including writing a book with her daughter, Chelsea, called *The Book of Gutsy Women: Favorite Stories of Courage and Resilience*. Thanks to the attempts (and failures) of Hillary Clinton and many others like her, more women were elected to public office in 2018 than at any other point in U.S. history.

Failing, Flailing, and Flying

Time to celebrate! At this point in life, you've made many mistakes and have experienced failure—because you're human. You're a learner, and you've stepped into your learning and growth zones time after time. Have you designed a way to celebrate your mistakes and failures yet?

TRY THIS! A NEW KIND OF HIGH FIVE

How might you celebrate your mistakes and failures? When I was in college, my best friend Stacey introduced me to self-high fives. Whenever she was excited about something, she gave herself a high five. Self-high fives may sound silly, but I've grown to love them. When I make a mistake, in my mind I give myself a high five.

What are some ways you can celebrate your mistakes and failures? List three ways.

WE MAY ENCOUNTER

MANY
DEFEATS

BUT WE MUST

NOT BE
DEFEATED.

—MAYA ANGELOU

CHAPTER SIX
ON A ROLL

Taking on new challenges is empowering and exciting. But it isn't always easy! Sometimes when we meet a whole lot of resistance, we want to give up or turn in another direction. And when resistance shows up, lots of thoughts and emotions do, too.

But, like mistakes, thoughts and emotions are just information to learn from: Are they trying to warn you about something? Keep you safe? Or are they trying to keep you in your comfort and fear zones? Are they holding you back, or are they encouraging you to learn and grow?

In this chapter, you'll work on how to embrace resistance while listening hard to your inner voice. You'll examine what your inner voice is really trying to tell you and use this information to navigate any obstacle in front of you.

Frustration Means It's Working

Growth mindset helps you take on challenges and try new things because that's where learning and brain stretching happen.

Yet, as you take on a challenge and try something new, frustration usually steps in. That's how you know it's a challenge to begin with! You experience frustration and struggle because you are moving out of your comfort zone. This is totally normal! Frustration means you are in your learning and growth zones. Struggle and frustration are signs you are learning.

The next time you're learning something new and you start to experience thoughts and feelings of struggle and frustration, try one of these techniques:

* Take some deep breaths.

* Focus on your courage mantras.

* Pay attention to your thoughts and emotions. What are you thinking? What are you feeling?

* Acknowledge your thoughts and emotions: "I am feeling . . ." "I am thinking . . ."

After you get more comfortable checking in with your thoughts and emotions, see how you can change them to cause forward action. (Hint: See if you can use the magic of "yet.")

Here are some examples:

FRUSTRATED	FORWARD ACTION
"This is too hard."	"This is hard right now because it's new, but I know if I move with these feelings of struggle and frustration, I will get better at it."
"I don't know how to do this."	"I don't know how to do this yet, but when I do, I will feel proud of myself."
"I can't do this."	"I can't do this yet. I need time to study and practice, and then I will be better at it."
"Why is this person trying to stop me?"	"I wonder what they're afraid of. They must not know how to view me or themselves through a growth mindset yet."

Now it's your turn. In the left-hand column, write down three things you might feel when you are frustrated. In the right-hand column, turn these feelings of frustration into forward action.

FRUSTRATED	FORWARD ACTION

The Maybe Story

You know by now about the magic of "yet." But have you ever heard of the magic of "maybe"? Sometimes things will not go the way you think or plan—actually, that is usually the case for most people! Mistakes and failures will happen, and the need for do-overs will pop up all the time.

When these moments happen—especially when they happen in front of others—we start worrying about what others think about us. "Did they hear my voice shake during my presentation? Did they notice the pimple on my nose?" These thoughts are totally normal. We are social beings, so we pay attention to what others think.

However, the truth is that we really don't *know* what others think, and just as our thoughts are temporary, so are theirs. This is where "maybe" comes in. "Maybe people were so involved in their own thoughts that they didn't even hear my voice shake." Or "maybe they noticed the pimple on my nose and thought about it for like one nanosecond and then moved on to their next fleeting thought: what they need to finish on their project or whether their little brother took their gum or who they need to text after school or talk to at lunch or . . . " You get the idea.

Remember: Thoughts and emotions are temporary—your own and others'.

Focus on Things You Can Control

There are many things in our lives that we can control and many things that we simply cannot. The weather? Nope. Other people's thoughts and opinions about you? Nope. Our thoughts and opinions about ourselves? Yep. Our respect, kindness, and compassion toward ourselves? Yep.

There are times in life when you may feel out of control or that you are losing control. That's totally normal. This may happen particularly if you start worrying about what others may think or feel about you. In these moments, it's important to get back to your center, to your inside world.

When you feel out of control, slow down and take a few deep breaths. Next, direct your attention and focus to the things you *can* control. Use these questions to help redirect your focus.

* What parts of my body do I want to move?

* What do I want to think about?

* What song do I want to sing or hum?

* What do I want to design and create?

* What do I want to dream about?

* What else is in my control?

Use the space that follows to answer any one of these questions. Return to them as often as you need.

Change Is Good

Change is happening all around us, all the time. Change creates new skies to look at, new seasons to experience, new thoughts and ideas to explore, new friends to spend time with, new experiences to enjoy, and new opportunities for learning and growth.

Welcoming our mistakes and failures, taking on challenges, problem-solving, and learning all cause changes—literal changes in the organization of our brains as well as changes in our thinking, feeling, and being. We are always becoming.

In her book *Becoming,* former First Lady Michelle Obama shares much of what she's learned, including how she realized we adults were sending limiting messages by asking one particular question over and over: "Now I think it's one of the most useless questions an adult can ask a child—*What do you want to be when you grow up?* As if growing up is finite. As if at some point you become something and that's the end."

Her book's title refers to the idea that we are always changing and evolving. During life's journey, there isn't some set point when we suddenly stop learning, changing, and growing. We are always becoming.

If someone asks you what you want to be when you grow up, you might feel resistance. You might even feel shame if you don't know the answer. That's a normal reaction! But as Michelle Obama tells us, it's a silly question to begin with!

Instead of thinking about what you want to be, consider how you want to treat people. As the saying goes, "They may forget what you said—but they will never forget how you made them feel."

List five ways you want to treat people.

Dream Bigger, Shine Brighter

This guide is all about learning how to use our growth mindset to access and celebrate our unlimited power and potential, even when the going gets tough. Following the growth mindset, you:

* Take ownership of your learning and growth. It's yours to nurture and cultivate, like a garden.

* Understand that learning takes effort and energy.

* Embrace challenges.

* Understand the value of mistakes.

* Never stop believing in your power, potential, and possibilities.

But what about when others doubt us, bully us, or don't understand who we are or how to support us along our way? Our growth mindset inspires us to dream bigger and shine brighter. So, it's important to remember that when someone sends you a message to dim your light, that's when you have to shine brighter. They can wear sunglasses if your light is too bright for them.

SHE GOT GRIT!

Jazz Jennings knew that her true self had the mind, heart, and soul of a girl—not a boy, which was what society saw her as. When she was six years old, she exercised her courage and bravery by doing an interview on this topic with the famous journalist Barbara Walters for a television special on **transgender** children.

Jazz continues to exercise her courage and bravery as an **LGBTQ+** activist, educating the world about her journey through her docuseries about her life and her children's book, both titled *I Am Jazz*, and her many speaking engagements around the world. She was named one of *Time* magazine's most influential teens in 2014 and 2015.

Putting Things into Perspective

Paying attention to and understanding what's happening in the world around you is a gift of being human. This awareness is an opportunity to allow your perspective and empathy to grow.

Empathy happens when you understand and are sensitive to the thoughts and emotions someone else is experiencing.

When you look around, you will see people living many different kinds of lives. You will see people in lives that they had a part in designing, and you will see people in lives that were designed for them. You will see problems, both big and small, and many opportunities to help. The problems in the world around us are opportunities to make meaningful change, opportunities to design and live our own fullest lives—and support others as they design and live theirs.

Take a moment to think about all that's happening around you. What's happening in your neighborhood? In your community? In your country? In the world? What are you seeing? Hearing? Feeling? Write some of your observations here.

What are some ways you can help others, maybe in your neighborhood or community, based on your observations?

Setting Goals Puts You in Charge

Okay, so what do you do with all this learning you're doing and the growth you're experiencing? You celebrate by taking action to grow even more. What does this mean? You can start by setting goals for yourself.

What is a goal, exactly? A goal is a specific idea for something you would like to achieve. A goal can be small or big. It's not about mapping out your whole life right now but instead about everyday actions you want to take to get you where you want to go.

Here are a few goal-setting ideas to get you started:

* Set a goal to celebrate yourself every day. Smile at yourself in the mirror.

* Set a goal to talk with others about what you've learned.

* Set a goal to learn something new.

* Set a goal to take on a new challenge.

* Set a goal to celebrate your next mistake.

* Set a goal to create a safe space for your classmate to celebrate their next mistake.

Now it's your turn. List goals you want to set for yourself. It helps to meet these goals if you also write down *when* you hope to complete your goal and who might help you get there. Remember: Goals are made to be revisited. Revision is part of the learning process!

MY GOAL	WHEN I WANT TO COMPLETE IT	WHO I'LL ASK FOR HELP

It's also okay when you don't meet your goal. Remember Serena Williams? Be curious about why you didn't achieve your goal. What got in your way? Maybe you didn't have the resources or support you needed, or maybe you came across others' limited messages blaring into your ear. Use that information to adjust your plan, then ask a trusted and supportive adult for what you need—and try again. Feel free to make some notes about your learning process.

NEVER CEASE
TO ACT
BECAUSE
YOU FEAR
YOU MAY FAIL.

—QUEEN LILIUOKALANI

CHAPTER SEVEN
GIRLS BREAKING BARRIERS

How does the experience of other women and girls relate to you and your ability to experience new things?

Throughout history, some people have had limited ideas about what girls and boys could and should do. Those in power decided that girls should do, learn, and feel some things and boys should do, learn, and feel other things. How silly! Because of these narrow ideas, people have closed off certain spaces, experiences, and opportunities to girls—especially girls of color.

Today we know society had (and often still has) a fixed mindset. Not only are girls and boys of all colors equal when it comes to what they can do, feel, and learn, but we also know that to tell someone what they can or should do based on their **sex** (their designation based on biological attributes), **gender** (how they identify), race, or any other characteristic hurts everyone. Boys cry and girls are loud! Girls wear blue, and boys love makeup, too. Boys grow up to be nurses, and girls grow up to found engineering companies. All of our brains are limitless.

The remnants of these old beliefs still impact boys and girls today, but we are getting better at debunking some of these false ideas. Let's take a look . . .

Myth Busting

One false story we've said goodbye to is that girls and women are not good at math, science, and technology. The truth? Girls and women have always been excellent mathematicians, scientists, and technologists. *Always*. Why? Because women and men have the same ability to learn.

Today we are in the process of discovering all of the ways that girls and women made their impact—even when they were not given credit.

Who was the first computer programmer? Who figured out the math formula that launched rockets into space? Who discovered and shared the first signs of neuroplasticity with the public? Who made major research advancements that cracked the mystery of human DNA? Women did—read on to learn more.

THEY GOT GRIT!

Ada Lovelace published the algorithm designed to be used by the first modern computer. She is known worldwide as the first computer programmer.

Katherine Johnson figured out the math formula that launched rockets into space, helping NASA send astronauts to orbit around the Earth, touch down on the moon, and return safely! Even though she faced **sexism** and **racism** at work, she never gave up. She loved math so much, people called her a computer.

Marian Diamond is considered one of the founders of modern neuroscience. She was the first to show the brain's neuroplasticity. She even discovered evidence of neuroplasticity in Albert Einstein's brain.

Rosalind Franklin's research led to new discoveries about human DNA, including proving that the structure of our DNA was a double helix. Even though two male scientists took credit for her work, she is considered one of the most inspirational scientists in history.

Going Way Back

Coming up against old, outdated, and inaccurate models can be sad and disappointing. But times are changing. Some might even say we're looking further back in history for examples of times when women were revered or deeply respected for inspiration.

You might have heard of the well-known Egyptian pharaoh Cleopatra, who ruled ancient Egypt. But did you know that she was not the first or only female pharaoh? A woman by the name of Hatshepsut, a word that means "foremost of noblewomen," was the first female leader of Egypt from 1473 to 1458 BCE. Understanding more about history can help us be part of the change that celebrates girls and boys equally. In fact, reading and studying this guide and using your knowledge to make meaningful contributions is a great start to becoming part of this change!

The Sky Is Not the Limit

Need more evidence of change? Less than one hundred years ago, we could not travel into space. But in 1969, Americans landed on the moon—thanks to Katherine Johnson's math skills! Even at this time of discovery, many people wrongly thought that women could not be astronauts. On October 18, 2019, the first all-women spacewalking team traveled into space to fix a broken part of the International Space Station's power grid. Many middle schoolers like you cheered on astronauts Christina Koch and Jessica Meir with signs that read, "The sky is not the limit!"

Today, six women and eight men are set to land on the moon in 2024 as part of the Artemis mission. These will be the first women on the moon—and they may go to Mars, too!

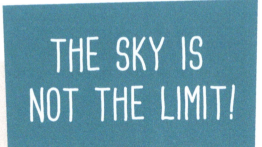

SHE GOT GRIT!

Want to build a rocket to take people to Mars? When she was a college student, rocket scientist Tiera Guinn Fletcher did just that. She contributed to NASA's biggest and most powerful rocket ever made. Today, Tiera works for Boeing, the largest aeronautics producer in the world.

Tiera grew up loving math and science, but reaching for her dreams and the stars wasn't always easy. She wanted to build planes and rockets, so she went to a high school that was an hour away because she knew it would help her reach her goals. She was often the only girl in her college aerospace and engineering classes—but none of that stopped her.

"You have to look forward to your dream and you can't let anybody get in the way of it. No matter how tough it may be, no matter how many tears you might cry, you have to keep pushing. And you have to understand that nothing comes easy. Keeping your eyes on the prize, you can succeed."

Take Up Space!

If you're actively increasing your power, potential, and possibilities in an attempt to reach your dreams, chances are you will find yourself in spaces where you are one of the only girls (or *the* only girl). Have you found this to be true?

While girls and boys are equally capable of learning, they don't always get the same support to enter these spaces. That's why confidence, courage, and leadership are so important. It's also important to know who your supporters are and to ask for their help.

If you feel like you're the only one asking for something, doing something, advocating for something, or pushing for something, that can feel lonely. But stretching yourself doesn't open more doors only for you; it leaves those doors open for all the girls who want to enter behind you. Don't be afraid to take up this space! It's your right.

> *"Courage is like—it's a habitus, a habit, a virtue: You get it by courageous acts. It's like you learn to swim by swimming. You learn courage by couraging."*
>
> —MARY DALY, THE FIRST AFRICAN AMERICAN WOMAN TO EARN A PHD IN CHEMISTRY

When you feel lonely, try reminding yourself that while you may not see other girls in the room, that doesn't mean it's not happening. They are out there pursuing their own goals, all over the world. Reading about the boundary-breaking achievements of girls and women will help you see that you are part of a powerful global movement. You can instantly feel proud of what you're doing—and feel a kinship with all of these amazing women and girls.

When you are feeling alone, remember this guide. Come back to this section. Read it again. Bookmark it. Dog-ear it and find this message: **YOU ARE NOT ALONE.**

I've got your back, and millions of other girls and women do, too. I guarantee it.

Global Girls

So many girls and young women around the world are doing brave things, everyday things to make their lives, their families, their schools, and their communities better—things to make the world better. How we each do these brave things looks different, and no one way is better than another. The resources we have available to us and the opportunities that come our way are different. How we organize our families and how we live our daily lives look different.

What we have in common is the motivation to be seen, heard, safe, respected, appreciated, valued, supported, and challenged. What do we want? The freedom to use and expand our power, to live our fullest life the way *we* see fit.

THEY GOT GRIT!

Girls and young women are leading climate change action. Most notable is Greta Thunberg, who was named *Time* magazine's 2019 Person of the Year. At sixteen, Greta sailed halfway around the world to speak in front of the entire world at the United Nations on behalf of climate change, a cause she cares deeply about. Because of this passion, she works tirelessly to lead this important charge.

Other girls want to fight climate change, too. They are speaking up, working together, and taking action. Isra Hirsi, Haven Coleman, and Alexandria Villaseñor co-founded the U.S. Youth Climate Strike, an organized walkout from schools to raise awareness of the impact of climate change. Sixteen-year-old Jamie Margolin, along with her friends Nadia Nazar, Madelaine Tew, and Zanagee Artis, started Zero Hour, a growing movement that organizes marches, festivals, summits, and the sharing of various resources and tools via social media.

You are living during a time when more and more young people—especially girls—are inspiring and creating change. Rapid change! How are you going to exercise your power, expand your potential, and grab hold of new possibilities? The time is now. Go for it!

Write down one thing you think needs to change in our culture or in the world.

Is there an action you can take tomorrow? Write down one small step you can take to ignite this change. Remember, Greta Thunberg started a global climate change revolution by staging a protest—one girl with one sign—in front of Swedish parliament.

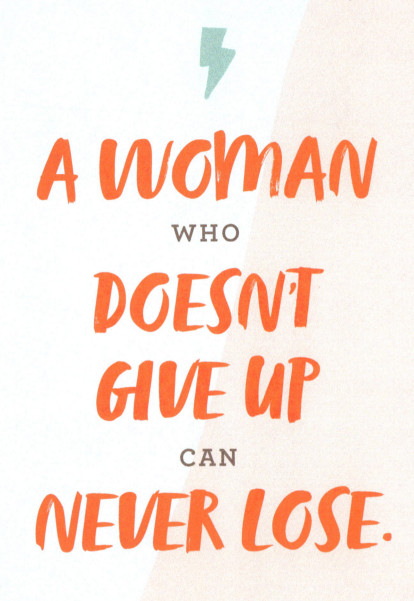

A WOMAN WHO DOESN'T GIVE UP CAN NEVER LOSE.

—ABBY WAMBACH

CHAPTER EIGHT

YOU AND YOUR WOLFPACK

One of the most magical experiences we have as humans is when we connect with people in honest and meaningful ways. When we show up as our whole selves, we are being real. We call this **authenticity**.

Authenticity means we are being our true selves in a given moment or situation—not who we think others want us to be or who others might like better. When you are authentic, you don't compromise your opinions, goals, ideas, hopes, dreams, or desires to please someone else. You don't sacrifice your own happiness to satisfy someone else's expectations of who you are. You don't compare yourself to others.

Being true to your authentic self is one of the hardest lessons you will learn. It takes bravery to honor who you are! And sometimes it takes a whole lifetime to get there. But it's the only way to find peace in yourself and form true, lasting relationships with those around you. Let's see all the ways you can tap into your growth mindset to develop your most authentic self.

Your Freest Self

Who are you when you feel free—free to just be? Do you feel silly? Funny? Curious? Angry? Sad? Joyful? Annoyed? Frustrated? The key to growing your authentic self is to get in touch with your emotions. When you check in with your emotions, it becomes easier to just *be*. Know that whatever you are feeling and thinking now is both real and temporary. You feel it, so that makes it real. (No one can say that what you feel isn't real!) But it will pass and maybe return again. That's the nature of things: They come and go.

Showing up with our whole selves means we let go of judgment. We don't categorize what we feel or who we are as "good" or "bad." We just *are*. We also let go of judgment from others—the silent kind and the noisy kind. We're not comparing ourselves to others, wishing we could have what they have, look like they look, or do what they do.

It can feel uncomfortable to show up as your whole self because there are so many rules for how you are supposed to show up. These rules are made-up, and they limit you. Even the words "supposed to" are limiting.

In the left-hand column, write down five rules girls are "supposed to" follow. In the right-hand column, write a way to break each of these so-called rules. These are your new rules.

SO-CALLED RULE	BREAKING THE RULE
Girls should be nice and quiet.	Girls are free to be bold, loud, and brave.

Let's do the same thing for the rules boys are "supposed to" follow. These rules hurt all sexes and genders.

SO-CALLED RULE	BREAKING THE RULE
Boys should never cry.	Boys have powerful feelings and can cry all they want!

Bravery Is a Daily Practice

Designing and living your own life requires confidence, bravery, and courage. While this is very exciting, it isn't always easy! Every day that we practice our confidence, bravery, and courage, we cause them to grow. Here are some examples of ways you can practice confidence, bravery, and courage in your daily life. Feel free to share them with your family and friends!

* Show up as your true self—not some pretend version of yourself! Note: This might change depending on where your journey takes you and how you grow. Sometimes we can outgrow our old selves!

* Share your thoughts and opinions. Your ideas and your voice matter.

* Ask questions.

* Answer questions.

* Tell someone how you are feeling or how they hurt your feelings.

* Say "no" to something you don't want to do.

* Say "yes" to something you want to do but may feel nervous, scared, or anxious about! Ask questions as you make your decision about whether to follow through.

* Respect yourself.

* Respect others.

* Celebrate yourself.

* Celebrate others.

* Listen to yourself.

* Listen to others.

* Stick up for yourself.

* Stick up for others.

* Support yourself.

* Support others.

* Step outside your comfort zone.

* Try something new.

* Take on challenges.

* Learn from your mistakes.

* Make your own choices and decisions.

Write down three brave things you do on a daily basis. It can be something brave, like standing up to a bully, or something meaningful, like telling your teacher you need help.

Now, focus on one brave thing you will try before the end of the week. Imagine yourself trying it, making mistakes, and sticking with it. Write down this new act of bravery and what it feels like to take a risk!

Your Wolfpack

When you show up as your authentic self, you invite others to do the same. And when we all show up as our true and whole selves, magic happens. We connect with others and find ways to support, lift up, and celebrate each other. It's a special moment when we turn individual support into group support.

One example of turning individual support into group support is found on the soccer field. In fact, professional soccer player and women's advocate Abby Wambach has a special name for it. She calls this type of collective support "rushing and pointing."

Abby knows that when she scores a goal, she does so because of her team. So, after she scores a goal, she and her teammates all "rush and point." Teammates rush toward the goal-scorer, and while they cheer for each other in a huddle, the goal-scorer points to her teammates, saying, "Because of you, I just scored this goal!" Rushing and pointing celebrates teamwork, recognizes that success is best when it's shared, and lifts everybody up. It is what girl power is made of.

Abby's New Rules

In Abby's book, *Wolfpack: How to Come Together, Unleash Our Power, and Change the Game*, she's rewritten eight old rules:

OLD RULE	ABBY'S NEW RULE
Stay on the path.	Create your own path.
Be grateful for what you have.	Be grateful for what you have AND demand what you deserve.
Wait for permission to lead.	Lead now—from wherever you are.
Failure means you're out of the game.	Failure means you're finally IN the game.
Be against each other.	Be FOR each other.
Play it safe. Pass the ball.	Believe in yourself. Demand the ball.
Lead with dominance.	Lead with humanity. Cultivate leaders.
You're on your own.	You're not alone. You've got your pack.

Are any of Abby's rules similar to the ones you wrote previously? Feel free to use and adapt any and all of Abby's rules. She is part of your wolfpack!

SHE GOT GRIT!

Abby Wambach grew up playing soccer from the time she was four years old. She credits her older sisters and brothers with challenging her to become a better player. Yet in her teenage and adult life, Abby went through tough times. She faced prejudice for being gay, which led to pain and abuse. On the field, she suffered head injuries. With a growth mindset, Abby became her brightest self! She has two Olympic gold medals, holds the world record for the number of international goals scored, is a FIFA Women's World Cup champion, and a six-time winner of the U.S. Soccer Athlete of the Year award. Today, her advocacy for women and girls transcends the field.

Global Girl Power

Girls and women team up to support, lift up, and celebrate each other all over the world. We have so many powerful examples:

* Michelle Obama, Malala Yousafzai, and Oprah Winfrey advocating for girls' education around the world

* Melinda Gates advocating for gender equality and equity across continents

* Girls like Greta Thunberg joining forces to lead climate action

* Women's soccer teams led by players like Abby Wambach, Megan Rapinoe, and Alex Morgan fighting for equal pay

* Teachers working together to make sure they are well supported as they care for, teach, and support students and families

* Women activists like Gloria Steinem and Maria da Penha creating forums for women to learn, share, and demonstrate

* Political leaders like Stacey Abrams, Jacinda Ardern, and Cynthia Semíramis working together to elect more women to public office

When we support, lift up, and celebrate each other, there's nothing we can't do.

"We cannot all succeed when half of us are held back. We call upon our sisters around the world to be brave—to embrace the strength within themselves and realize their full potential."

—MALALA YOUSAFZAI

You might be supporting women and girls without even knowing it. It's important to celebrate yourself and the way you lift up others! Maybe you helped a friend with her math homework, encouraged two friends to work through a disagreement, went to your friend's first basketball game, or organized a group to go to the Women's March.

List two things you've done to support other girls or the women in your life.

1. _____

_____

2. _____

_____

Now, list two ways you can help girls around the world.

1. _____

_____

2. _____

_____

Changing Over Time

We've talked about how it's unfair to compare ourselves to others and how it's also unfair to compare ourselves to past versions of ourselves. Why? Because we are always changing and growing.

When we look inside us and around us, we can see that change is happening all the time within our inside and outside world. It's happening to us—and to everyone we know. It's even happening to plants and animals! What are some examples?

You are not the person you were five years ago, one month ago, or even one minute ago! List three ways you have changed over time. This can include new hobbies you took up, new ways of thinking, or acts of bravery that changed who you are.

Limitless You

In this guide, you learned how to increase your power, potential, and possibilities. And you made the world a better place. Time to celebrate again! Congratulate yourself because you just dedicated time and energy to making your internal strengths and resources grow.

Your power and potential are limitless, so imagine all the possibilities before you. You are learning, changing, growing— evolving your whole life. Learning has no age requirement and no age limit. So embrace it, celebrate it, and go forth to design and live your fullest life!

Together, let's dream bigger and shine brighter to make the world a better place!

A special note of thanks: Thank you for joining me on this journey. You all inspire me to design and live my fullest life, and I am grateful for each of you. Keep flying high.

MY NOTES

This is extra space for you to record your thoughts, emotions, ideas, hopes, dreams, struggles, mistakes, failures, and acts of resilience. This is your space. And it's as wild and free as you are.

GLOSSARY

abstract thinking: a way of thinking deeply about something that is not concrete or specific

amygdala: the part of the brain connected to emotional memories

antidote: something that relieves or counteracts

authenticity: the quality of being real and genuine

brain stem: the area at the base of the brain that sits between the two cerebral hemispheres and the cervical spinal cord

cerebellum: the part of the brain that regulates muscular activity

cerebrum: the part of the brain that integrates sensory and neural functions with involuntary body activity

comfort zone: a place where you feel safe and in control

concrete thinking: a way of thinking literally about the physical world

empathy: being aware of, understanding, and being sensitive to others' thoughts, feelings, and experiences

fear zone: a place where you feel scared or anxious and might want to withdraw from or avoid situations causing you anxiety

fear-based decisions: decisions made from fear that keep you in your comfort zone

feedback: information you get from the outside world, such as from friends

gender: the attitudes, feelings, and behaviors associated with a person's identity as male, female, or non-binary

growth mindset: our belief that our intelligence, abilities, skills, talents, and personality are malleable because the brain is malleable and neuroplastic. It's always changing and growing because of what we think, feel, say, experience, and do.

growth zone: a place where you use what you learn and set goals for yourself

growth-based decisions: decisions made from a place of growth, moving beyond fear

hippocampus: the part of the brain that is the center of emotion, memory, and the nervous system

learning zone: a place where you try new things, take risks, and learn

LGBTQ: an acronym for lesbian, gay, bisexual, transgender, and queer (or questioning)

malleable: having the capacity for change

mantra: a statement we repeat to ourselves in order to focus our internal energy on something

meditation: a mental exercise to train focus, attention, and awareness (for example, mindfulness is one possible meditation technique)

mindfulness: being aware of and living in the present moment—not what happened in the past nor what might happen in the future but RIGHT NOW

mindset: a set of mental attitudes you and others hold

neurogenesis: the process of growing new neurons

neurons: the main building material of the brain and nervous system. They carry information throughout the human body.

neuroplasticity: the ability of the brain to change throughout a person's life

neuroscience: the scientific study of the body's nervous system

neuroscientist: a person who is an expert in neuroscience

passion: something you deeply care about, value, and think is really important. This is something you want to spend more time doing.

performance zone: a place where you feel judged or evaluated or where you think mistakes and failure are unwelcome

perseverance: the attitude and ability to stick with something even when things or people get in your way, you struggle or fail at it, or you experience some other obstacle that distracts you

prefrontal cortex: the part of the brain that regulates choices, decisions, planning, and self-control

ruminating: to go over something in the mind repeatedly

self-limiting story: beliefs or stories we tell about ourselves that hold us back

self-talk: conversations we have with ourselves

sex: a person's biological status, assigned at birth based on a number of different biological traits; generally male, female, or intersex

transgender: a person whose gender identity is different from the sex they were assigned at birth (e.g., a trans man identifies as male but was assigned female at birth)

RESOURCES

Amy Poehler's Smart Girls aims to help young women with life's problems in a funny but informative way.

* *amysmartgirls.com*

Black Girls Code empowers young girls of color ages 7 to 17 to become innovators, leaders, and builders of their future through computer science and technology.

* *blackgirlscode.org*

Character Lab shares actionable advice for parents and teachers based on science. Founded by Angela Duckworth, the author of *Grit: The Power of Passion and Perseverance*.

* *characterlab.org*

Girls Who Code aims to close the gender gap in technology by offering learning opportunities for girls in computer science. Founded by Reshma Saujani, author of *Brave, Not Perfect: Fear Less, Fail More, and Live Bolder*.

* *girlswhocode.com*

Girls Write Now mentors underserved young women to find their voices through the power of writing and community.

* *girlswritenow.org*

Girls on the Run inspires girls to be joyful, healthy, and confident through experiences with integrating running.

* *girlsontherun.org*

Girls, Inc. inspires all girls to be strong, smart, and bold through direct service and advocacy.

* *girlsinc.org*

Girls Opportunity Alliance empowers adolescent girls around the world through education. Founded by former First Lady Michelle Obama.

* *girlsopportunityalliance.org*

Mindset Works is the global leader in growth mindset. Mindset Works promotes a growth mindset through research, partnerships, programs for students and educators, other tools and resources, and advocacy. Founded by Carol Dweck, author of *Mindset: The New Psychology of Success*, and colleagues Dr. Lisa Blackwell and Eduardo Briceño.

* *mindsetworks.com*

The Collaborative for Academic, Social, and Emotional Learning (CASEL) is the leading organization for social and emotional learning (SEL). CASEL promotes SEL through research, partnerships, tools and resources, and advocacy.

* *casel.org*

YouCubed brings growth mindset and mathematics together to inspire all students with open, creative mindset mathematics. Founded by Dr. Jo Boaler, author of *Mathematical Mindsets: Unleashing Students' Potential through Creative Math, Inspiring Messages, and Innovative Teaching* and *Limitless Mind: Learn, Lead, and Live without Barriers.*

* *youcubed.org*

Venture Lab empowers kids, especially girls, to innovate, create, and discover their potential. Founded by Cristal Glangchai, author of *Venture Girls: Raising Girls to Be Tomorrow's Leaders.*

* *venturelab.org*

Zero Hour centers the voices of diverse youth in the conversation around climate and environmental justice.

* *thisiszerohour.org*

PERIOD provides free, clean, and healthy period products to schools, shelters, and prisons. The organization educates people on how to change the way people think, talk, and learn about periods. Its organizers fight for system-wide change toward menstrual equity.

* *period.org*

A Mighty Girl is the world's largest collection of books, toys, and movies for confident and courageous girls.

* *amightygirl.com*

REFERENCES

Brown, Brené. *Braving the Wilderness: The Quest for True Belonging and the Courage to Stand Alone*. New York: Random House, 2017.

Boaler, Jo. *Limitless Mind: Learn, Lead, and Live without Barriers*. New York: HarperOne, 2019.

Boaler, Jo. "Mistakes Grow Your Brain." YouCubed. https://www.youcubed.org/evidence/mistakes-grow-brain.

Curry, Colleen. "17 Top Female Scientists Who Have Changed the World." Global Citizen. https://www.globalcitizen.org/en/content/17-top-female-scientists-who-have-changed-the-worl.

Duckworth, Angela. *Grit: The Power of Passion and Perseverance*. New York: Scribner, 2016.

Dweck, Carol. *Mindset: The New Psychology of Success*. New York: Ballantine Books, 2006. (*Source of the adapted Mindset Works chart used on page 5.)

Obama, Michelle. *Becoming*. New York: Crown, 2018.

Wambach, Abby. *Wolfpack: How to Come Together, Unleash Our Power, and Change the Game*. New York: Celadon Books, 2019.

INDEX

ACKNOWLEDGMENTS

I have had many women in my life who have taught, supported, and inspired me to be ME: my lifetime best friend from college, Stacey. My cousin Roberta. My aunt Janine, one of the original powerhouse women that I knew. So many loving, supportive, and inspiring friends, colleagues, and mentors. But the first woman who gave me wings to fly was my mom, Denise. Thank you, Mom; I keep flying higher and better because of you.

I had a very special editor and inspiration along the way, giving me honest feedback: my daughter, Rouene. Thank you, Rou, for being my teacher and inspiring me. I appreciate all your love, kindness, support, ideas, and suggestions. Keep flying!

To a young man who shows me every day what gentleness and kindness feel like and reminds me to play: my son, Rieder. Keep flying!

Thank you to the loving and supportive men in my life: my dad, who always directed the wind my way so I could fly faster and higher. My brothers, who knew I was flying and never got in my way. And Trevor, who gave me support along the way.

Thank you to all my fellow creative, brave, and bold educators and friends who continue to advocate, challenge, and inspire us all to do and be better. I love you all. A special gratitude shout-out to all our Growing Early Mindsets (GEM) teachers! You know who you are. You bring growth mindset and social and emotional learning (SEL) to life every day by creating conditions and opportunities for future generations to thrive.

A special thanks to the women at Jackson's Corner, who continue to be a source of warmth, strength, and inspiration!

Thank you to all my students (and girls basketball players) over the years from preschool to adult. Together we learn and grow.

Thank you to the Mindset Works team for your steadfast dedication to promoting a growth mindset for all. Over the years, you all have served as energy and inspiration as I continue in the field to promote, teach, foster, and apply a growth mindset even when we meet resistance. Thank you, Carol Dweck and Lisa Blackwell, for leading the way.

And thank you to Erin Nelson, my editor, and her whole team, who knew this book had to be written, brought to life, and shared.

Cheers to all of us celebrating our unlimited power, potential, and possibilities!

ABOUT THE AUTHOR

Kendra Coates, D.Ed, loves to learn. She was once a young girl and woman like you and would have loved to read this book. She travels around the country sharing the power and potential of neuroscience, growth mindset, social and emotional learning (SEL), and mindfulness with anyone who will listen—and sometimes even with those who may not want to listen yet. In her many years in education, she has taught all ages, from preschool to middle school to college to professionals. She's learning all the time as a human on our planet through her many roles of learner, mom, teacher, writer, speaker, leader, and entrepreneur. Follow her on Twitter and Instagram at @DrKendraCoates. You can visit her at upbydesign.org.